This book is dedicated to the memory of Mike Lee Brown, agent to Dabo Swinney and dear friend to Clemson University. Mike Brown passed away on January 29, 2017, following a battle with cancer. Throughout his career as a sports agent, Mike touched the lives of players, coaches, and support staff. Mike was the driving force behind many initiatives for Clemson football, most notably the creation of Dabo Swinney's All In Team Foundation. He was a humble man who worked largely behind the scenes, but left a lasting legacy for Clemson football. He will be deeply missed by the entire Clemson family, but his impact will endure for generations.

www.mascotbooks.com

It's Gameday in Death Valley!

For more information, please contact:
Mascot Books
560 Herndon Parkway #120
Herndon, VA 20170
info@mascotbooks.com

CPSIA Code: PBANG0517A
ISBN-13: 978-1-68401-053-0

Printed in the United States

Photo credit: Allen Randall

It's Gameday
in Death Valley!

by Julie Smart

A is for Alma Mater,

Sing with all our might:

"That the tiger's roar may echo

O'er the mountain height."

B is for pre-game buses,

Our Tigers packed inside.

As they round the corner,

The fans all cheer with pride.

The Cadence Count will echo

Mixed with the tiger's roar.

The crowd is getting louder now,

We yell "One-two-three-four!"

Defense takes the field now,

Aiming for a sack.

Stopping our opponents

To get the football back.

Photo credit: Carl Ackerman

End zone, that's the target,

Short pass or run outside.

Fighting past defenders

To get the ball inside.

Photo credit: Julie Smart

Playing on **F**rank Howard Field,

Nestled in the Valley,

Decades of our Tigers

Have gathered here to rally.

It's Game day here in Clemson!

Fans come from far and wide.

We gather in the Valley,

All filled with Tiger pride.

The buses round the corner,

Our Tigers crest the Hill,

Cannons boom and cheers erupt,

The Valley's greatest thrill!

Photo credit: Rex Brown

I is interception,

A pass that got away.

Instead of the receiver,

Our defense makes the play.

Photo credit: Rex Brown

J is for jerseys,

All dressed for the challenge.

Away we wear white,

But at home, solid orange.

K is for kicker,

The ball soars through the uprights.

A game-winning field goal

Could land in the highlights!

Photo credit: Carl Ackerman

L is for linebacker,

Our defensive leaders.

They're defending the run

And covering receivers.

Photo credit: Allen Randall

M is for marching band

Under color guard flags.

Filling the Valley

With the ole' Tiger Rag.

N is for National Champions!

Tigers win the title!

Scoring in the final seconds

To defeat a mighty rival!

Photo credit: Carl Ackerman

O is for offense,

Explosive and quick.

Runs and deep passes

Keep moving the sticks!

We meet at the Paw

After every home game.

Whatever the outcome,

United the same.

Photo credit: Carl Ackerman

Q is for quarterback,

Young fans wear their numbers.

From Watson to Boyd,

The crowd cheers and thunders.

Photo credit: Rex Brown

Rubbing the Rock,

A long Clemson tradition.

The team gathers there,

With arms locked in unison.

Photo credit: Allen Randall

§ is for students,

The heartbeat of game time.

Rocking the south stands

And flooding the hill side.

T is for Tiger Walk,

Our newest tradition.

Flanked by fans on all sides,

Tigers march to the West End.

U is for upper deck,

Fans ascend row by row.

Their loud cheers rain down,

On the Valley below.

V is for visiting team,

Journeys short; journeys long.

Greeted in the Valley

By 80,000 fans strong.

W is for **W**est End Zone,

Standing tall and bright.

When the Tigers score a touchdown,

Fireworks light up the night!

Photo credit: Carl Ackerman

X is for x-ray,

A player's worst fear.

That a hit on the gridiron

Can end his whole year.

Photo credit: Craig Mahaffey

10 Yards to first down,

Hallmark of our sport.

Games have been won and lost

By falling just short.

Photo credit: Carl Ackerman

Zzzz, Tiger Nation

Sleeps soundly tonight,

With victory lullabies

And a future that's bright.

About the Author

Julie Smart is a teacher educator, educational researcher, and author. She currently teaches in the education department at Clemson University. She holds a Ph.D. in Curriculum and Instruction and regularly publishes in both teacher practitioner journals and national and international research journals. Julie specializes in math and science education and began her career as a public school teacher in her hometown of Greenville, South Carolina. Julie lives in Greenville with her husband, Andrew, a former Clemson football player, and her Irish twins, Drew and Claire. Julie and Andrew are avid supporters of Clemson's football program and Dabo Swinney's All In Team Foundation.

Have a book idea?
Contact us at:

info@mascotbooks.com | www.mascotbooks.com